# Life as I know it

A wee book of poems

By

V J Cooper

To Lynda,
Best Wishes,
V.J. Cooper

Published by First Spark Publishing



A CIP catalogue record for this book is available from the British Library.

ISBN 978-1-7394501-3-7 (paperback)

# Contents

# One in a million

I think of my quirks and my own way of being,
my thoughts and my dreams and my mind.
The home where I live and the people I love,
and those I have yet to find.
The memories I hold, that are mine alone,
most of which comfort, and others that don't.
The skills that I have and the things I've achieved,
Belong to no other than me.
The choices I've made and the road I have walked,
Have made me the person you see.
To be one in a million would be common indeed,
And that is not what we should seek.
If you look at me closely I hope that you see,
I'm not one in a million, I'm unique!

# My Mark

If I made my mark in pencil would someone rub
me out?

Would I just disappear and leave them with no
doubt,

that my life was insignificant with no worth in it at
all?

That I had no right to be here and seen as very
small?

Or would that mark just fade away, slowly over
time,

With no one really noticing that I was in my
prime?

The paper once so crisp and white, now yellowed
and all torn,

The cover lying in tatters and the spine, old and
very worn.

Perhaps I would be lifted and held up to the light,

Where I could be seen and heard, a whisper in the night,

My words and my behaviour signifying a life,

of love, of grief, of fun, of hope – a daughter, a mum, a wife.

To be held up and acknowledged: to be read,

Would allow the life within me to shine and not be shed,

But I chose to use a pencil, the pen is not for me,

I like that it will fade in time, this life that is to be.

The mark I make belongs to me, my life is mine alone,

and those who hold me in their hearts is where I make my home,

My words may fade and falter, my cover may well age,

but you'll always find me nestled warmly on the page.

# Your companion

Growing up with death as your companion,

A shadow that walks beside you every day,

Plants a seed of fear of losing those you love,

Of everyone you know being taken away.

The child you are has no understanding,

Of why so many people end up dead,

It's just how your life is and you accept it,

But it's frightening and fills your mind with dread.

One day you have a thought that maybe it's your fault,

That maybe there's a curse inside of you,

That maybe you're responsible for all these people dying,

That maybe you are bad and this is what you do.

As the years go by and you grow older,

You begin to understand that people die,

Not because of you but because they are unlucky,

They fall ill and have to leave you, and you cry.

But even though you understand it now,

That seed of fear, its roots run deep within,

You hold your loved ones close but the shadow's always there,

You go through life with death as your companion.

# Is it normal?

I tried to be normal once. Worst two minutes of my life.

What is normal anyway? It only brings you strife.

Trying to emulate others, what they say and what they do,

Instead of being yourself and letting you just be you.

Is it normal to dislike coasters, and be afraid of cats,

To enjoy historical research and look up lots of facts,

To hate the taste of eggs, unless they're in a cake,

To cook a lovely meal, but not know how to bake?

Is it normal to be neither, a morning or night person,

When three o'clock in the afternoon is your favourite time for certain,

To enjoy a glass of wine but hate the taste of beer,

When Hogmanay upsets you, and to bed you disappear?

Is it normal to enjoy, both the country and the city,

That when you see a pet, it fills your heart with pity,

To have a sense of smell, so acutely strong,

That you can smell a ladybird, as it crawls along?

I tried to be normal once. Worst two minutes of my life.

There really was no fun in it, it only brought me strife,

So here I'll stay with all my quirks, my foibles and my ways,

They've been with me since the seventies, so I doubt they're just a phase.

# When all around

When all around is chaotic and loud, it's *your* voice I hear,

It whispers to me, soft in my ear,

When all around is chaotic and loud, it's *your* hand I feel,

It entwines in mine, strong as steel,

When all around is chaotic and loud, it's *your* eyes I see,

Their depth envelops and strengthens me,

When all around is chaotic and loud

It's you and me, there is no other sound.

# Life in my mid-twenties

Life in my mid-twenties when my confidence
knew no bounds,

When flirting was fun and exhilarating and I
danced to any sound,

A strong, independent woman, I chose how to live
my life,

I drank shots and danced on tables and partying
was my life.

I was chatted up, I was single, I was dated, I was
dumped,

I made both good and bad choices but into them all
I jumped,

I asked men out, I dumped them, I loved the thrill
of the chase,

The future had few plans in it and a smile lit up my
face.

I allowed others to behave badly but I also learned from that,

What I sought and what I needed, and not to be a mat,

I learnt too young how short life is, so I determined to live life to the full,

I followed my gut instincts and was as thrawn as any bull.

Learning how to kiss well is an absolute must in life,

And there are three rules to follow before you become a wife,

The head, the heart and the loins must always totally agree,

Two out of three isn't good enough. I am glad I listened to me.

I may not be in my twenties now, but I look back at my life in awe,

So much fun and laughter was had, and I was enriched by what I saw,

Time is both irrelevant and significant, and teaches us frequently,

I look back and smile, there are no regrets, it's where I learned to be me.

# I always make a list

When something needs to be done, I always make a list,

And I have to write it on a piece of paper.

Not for me the use of a computer or my phone,

They are too much of a faff, and nothing but a caper.

If I'm going away somewhere, I always make a list,

One for what to take, and one of things to do before I go,

And a separate one for kids,

Oh how the lists do grow.

When I go out for my messages, I always make a list (or a liney as it's known)

This is one I really hate to do,

It is so very boring buying food of which to eat,

I really would just rather clean the loo.

I write that list in order of where things are within the shop,

I imagine walking round it in my mind,

I need that list so that I don't forget what it is I need,

But it's funny how I never need to write down wine.

Whenever I need to make a list, I always make a list,

You see I need a list for the other list I make,

Without a list nothing would actually happen,

Without a list, I simply could not function.

# The daffodil

When summer passed in a haze

and autumn felt unbearable,

and winter numbed my grief,

spring brought the daffodil outside my door.

It made me pause and take a breath.

I wondered if it was lonely, as I was lonely,

but it stood so tall and proud and looked so beautiful,

that splash of vivid colour in a grey corner by the door.

I smiled.

I would be alright.

I would live and move towards another way of being:

an adult way, as childhood was now gone.

As I took that first new breath up my chin rose and straightened my back

And I walked to school – different: not healed, but better.

I could look to a future and take that daffodil with me,

Its petals enveloping Mam who lived in my heart.

# Salmon

I move with the tide, each wave tossing me this
way and that.

Like a salmon I may swim against the tide:
searching.

Inner feelings pitch and roll, crashing against the
ocean's storms.

One day the tide will turn and carry me to calm
waters,

But the search will end only when the water is still.

# I wonder

I wonder what it's like to travel with a circus,

I wonder what it's like to always have a purpose.

I wonder what it's like to sing upon the stage,

I wonder what it's like to see your parents reach old age.

I wonder what it's like to have friends in your life,

I wonder what it's like to have never known strife.

I wonder what it's like to be a criminal on the run,

I wonder what it's like to have borne a son.

I wonder what it's like to have a holiday,

I wonder what it's like to live very far away.

I wonder what it's like to find a piece of gold,

I wonder what it's like to become very old.

# Our language holds no word

To look upon our newborn child, evokes a depth of feeling,

So strong, its power it has no name, but is itself revealing,

It shows that in an instant, our emotions can be so strong,

To love another instantly, and be where we belong.

A yearning that was deep inside, is now in the world,

The petals of our happiness, have suddenly unfurled,

Revealing both a softness, as love engulfs our hearts,

And a fierce protectiveness, that being a parent imparts.

In those first few moments, nothing else exists,

We are cocooned within a bubble, shrouded in a mist,

Oblivious of others, of time completely unaware,

All we see before us is our baby, whom we share.

Our language holds no word, to describe that first meeting,

Perhaps one word is not enough, to encapture the full meaning,

So for now we sit and hold our child, in a warm embrace,

And revel in our feelings, as we look upon her bonny face.

# What's the point o' coasters?

What's the point o' coasters? They sit underneath your drink,

They make me absolutely mad, and drive me to the brink,

'Here you go,' I hear you say, 'Put this underneath,'

I politely do as I am asked, and staunchly grit my teeth.

And there it stays all mocking and sly, it taunts me with its presence,

It knows that I have no way, of acting out my vengeance,

It waits for me to take a sip, my drink then needs returning,

I need to fully concentrate, my insides are a churning.

I can't just gently place my drink, back upon the table,

Anywhere I want to, of which I'd be quite able,

No! I have to try and negotiate, the landing of my glass,

It has to sit precisely, or disaster will come to pass.

You see, coasters are notorious, for tripping up your drink,

*They* are to be feared, as they're scarier than you think,

One wrong move, your glass is doomed, and off it topples over,

Panic rises in my chest, but time will not go slower.

Time to catch the falling glass, as it teeters on the edge,

That damned coaster is too small, and will not heed my pledge,

I tried so hard to get it right, I was a sniper with a target,

Now I watch in horror, as my drink lands on the carpet.

I glower at you, coaster, this is all your fault,

If I had my way, you'd be locked up in a vault,

Never to be seen again, never again to mock,

Never to be taken out when it's wine o'clock.

What's the point o' coaster? Work of the devil they be!

But now I have the upper hand, I have a plan you see,

Instead of placing down my drink. I'll hold it in my hand,

You can stay there all alone, Coaster, you be damned!

# What's the point o' running?

What's the point o' running? I've never understood,

Unless you're being chased, by a crook up to no good,

Or a dog that's out to get you, and bite you on the leg,

By all means run away, as you'd surely get a fleg.

Are you running to or from, when you take yourself out running?

Or do you run round in a circle, not knowing if you're going or coming?

It just always looks so aimless, and no one ever smiles,

Just forcing your wee leggies and racking up the miles.

There appear to be two types of folk, you see who sprint along,

The first is dressed in all the gear, and their legs are going strong,

They're on a mission, a time to beat, and they're striding straight ahead,

They are focused and determined, no pain stops them in their stead.

The other type is struggling, their run is one of dread,

With sweat pouring from every pore, and a face that is bright red,

They force themselves to move their legs, in an awkward and painful way,

A look of desperation, it's the hell within their day.

They have one thing in common though, they share the same belief,

That running is good for them, and that comes as some relief,

It makes them keep on doing it, day after day after day,

Their brains are fixated, and they can see no other way.

Well! Let me tell you this, you folk who go for a run,

There are better ways to exercise, which are actually quite fun,

Use your legs for walking, enjoy the surroundings you can see,

Ditch the pain and anguish, therefore setting yourself free.

To get your heart rate up, and muscles to be flexed,

There is no better way, than time spent having sex,

You will still sweat profusely, and your face may well turn red,

It is much more fun to exercise, whilst spending time in bed.

What's the point o' running? There is no point at all,

So spare your knees and joints, no need to risk a fall,

Why go out when it's raining to stagger through a puddle,

When you can go to bed and have a little cuddle!

# What's the point o' worrying?

What's the point o' worrying? It does no good at all,

It causes you distress, as you're climbing up the wall,

You pace the floor in anguish, and your mind is going full pelt,

You imagine what could happen, if a bad hand you are dealt.

So take some time to sit, and allow yourself to breathe,

Let your mind relax, and have some time to ease,

The burden you are carrying, it does not serve you well,

There is no point in worrying, as only time will tell.

Often we are thinking, about things yet to come to pass,

These things may never happen and nothing ever lasts,

So what's the point o' worrying? Absolutely none,

Look at life another way and better times will come.

# What’s the point o’ pasta?

What’s the point o’pasta? I can’t understand the passion,

It has nothing in it your body wants, so is it merely fashion?

A tasteless, bland, so called foodstuff that folk prefer over tatties,

Yet not a vitamin or mineral within it, and you certainly can’t make any patties,

In order to make it edible you have to add a sauce,

As to the carbohydrate, I couldn’t give a toss!

We can get that from our tatties and loads more besides,

Look at all the nutrients our humble tattie provides,

Vitamin C for your body and B6 for your brain,

Potassium for your heart and nerves, and Magnesium we do gain,

Throw in a bit of Iron and some dietary fibre too,

Our tatties are magnificent, well goodness me, who knew?

So don’t go filling your belly with pasta that does little good,

Embrace the tatties on your plate that actually pass as food,

What’s the point o’ pasta? No point at all I say,

So reach instead for your tatties and healthy you will stay.

# What's the point o' ticking clocks?

What's the point o' ticking clocks? Tap tapping in your ear,

They kill the silence in a room, and fill your mind wi' fear,

You hear your life go ticking by, one second at a time,

And realisation hits you, that you're no longer in your prime.

It's worse if it's in front of you, atop the mantel piece,

You can see the time escaping, and feel your life decrease,

My God, it's so depressing, why do we have such clocks?

Which shout to us as if in glee, 'You'll soon be dead!' it mocks.

The clock might think that it's in charge, but you're the boss of you,

So grab your time by the scruff of its neck, and look at things anew,

What's the point o' ticking clocks? They show us we need to live,

So do just that, however you please, as time is relative.

# Scotland's anthem

The lone piper begins and there's a lump in the throat,

As pride rises up from the heart,

The words come out strong as they hold firm to the pride,

And nothing can prise them apart.

The song speaks of history and of land that is ours,

And tears threaten to trickle down cheeks,

As the rousing words full of passion are sung,

The lump grows bigger and emotion peaks.

The skirl of the pipes stirs the blood deep within,

A lament to those gone and a call to those here,

A sense of oneness and belonging,

To a land we hold dear.

Standing tall, head held high as each note ignites,

A fire in the belly and strengthens the mind,

A love of our country so deep in our hearts,

Where loyalty and steadfastness bind.

Some cannot sing – the throat strangling the words,

But dignity and honour flow through the veins,

The heart beats faster and the mind is sincere,

A united understanding and togetherness reigns.

Our anthem comes to an end and there's an almighty roar,

As hope rises up and spirits soar,

Together we stand, Never alone,

Scotland my country,

Scotland my home.

# Murrayfield

The atmosphere at Murrayfield, really is exciting,

Even if it's pouring rain, and the wind is biting,

The hope you feel within yourself, raises anticipation,

Giving rise to a mind, full of exhilaration.

The build-up of elation, as you wait for the game to start,

Really takes a toll, on an emotional heart,

You sing *Flower of Scotland*, with tears in your eyes,

The pride you feel soaring, high up to the skies.

And so the whistle blows, all eyes are on the ball,

The opposition have it but end up in a maul,

All endeavour, to stay upon their feet,

No one wants a penalty, to make the fans greet.

A scrum is awarded, the crowd all shout 'Heave!'
Scotland push forward, five points they can achieve,
The fans are in a frenzy, shouting, 'Come on boys!'
The thumping of our hearts, adding to the noise.

The ball is passed backwards, a second phase of play,
Russell kicks a blinder, now we're just ten metres away,
Both teams form a line out, and Scotland wins the ball,
The winger, Van der Merwe, lets out a passionate call.

The ball is thrown towards him and he catches it mid-air,
And does what he does best, running with speed and flair,

The crowd has now erupted, they watch the winger fly,

And down the ball is grounded, Scotland have a Try.

Murrayfield is on its feet, bellies are on fire,

Watching Scotland winning, is something to admire,

Now to the conversion, Russell aims between the posts,

Up the ball does soar, and between the two it coasts.

And so the game continues, with rucks and scrums and tackles,

Eighty minutes of highs and lows, the atmosphere it crackles,

With penalties and turnovers, oh the angst it does produce,

And hearts they just stop beating, when the ball goes loose.

To watch your team play rugby, live at Murrayfield,

Your heart goes through the wringer, and fever it does yield,

But there is no game quite like it, I would have it no other way,

Life is intoxicating, when watching Scotland play.

# An ode to the thistle

The thistle represents a true Scottish mind,

Where characters of both are inextricably entwined,

Both are hardy and thrawn with sharp prickles for protection,

But their beauty and grace attracts much affection,

The roots run deep from ancestors to soil,

Resilience and strength that no war can spoil,

Held up by pride, a quiet presence resides,

And a shared understanding of our land coincides,

So raise a glass to the thistle, Caledonia we roam,

Sláinte Mháth, Scotland, our land and our home.

# Our national animal

The Unicorn is Scotland's national animal,

It is pure and innocent, yet strong and powerful,

With a history steeped in Celtic mythology,

And long ago tales of dominance and chivalry,

It represents the spirit of Scotland,

Which flows through our blood and seeps into our land.

# To the man in the kilt

To the man in the kilt who makes my heart beat faster,

No, not you – yours is a disaster!

You have not learnt that less is more,

That when you kneel down, your kilt must skim the floor,

Any longer in length it becomes a skirt,

And my feelings of likeness, you will hurt,

And look at your socks, an absolute disgrace,

They're far too high, heading towards your face!

Take them down from the knee to sit on top of the calf,

For goodness sake sort them, before others laugh,

There should be a gap between kilt and sock,

Measure six inches or others will mock,

Now where on earth are your laces going?

They're strung up your leg, what are you doing?

Get them down round your ankles, following seven twists,

Surely by now you get the gist,

Now to your jacket, the arms are too long,

The shirt should be visible so yours is just wrong,

And for goodness sake straighten your tie,

I am going to scream, no word o' a lie.

Here's the man in the kilt who makes my heart beat faster,

All is as it should be, he is a master,

His kilt's the right length, the socks the right height,

His laces are grand and winna take flight,

I can see his shirt cuffs and his tie is straight,

Oh my! He doesn't half look great,

He stands straight and proud, a true Scotsman is he,

Aren't I the lucky one as he's with me,

As he offers me his arm I turn all a quiver,

I catch a glimpse of his braces which cause me to shiver,

There is nothing sexier than a man in a kilt,

Especially those braces which make my heart tilt,

So to those who get it wrong, sort yourselves out,

Follow the rules and there'll be no doubt,

Women will come flocking with all their graces,

But don't disappoint – wear those braces!

# Thomas

No more for him the sound of screams

As shells and bullets mutilated,

No more for him the stench of death

Or lice and rats and fear,

A boy – clad in soldiers cloth, that cloth now shed as he lies dead.

He was but fodder.

Hear him whisper in the wind,

His voice forever young,

And speak his name so he will be remembered.

The seasons pull the years along, as nature must,

But time must not steal,

Those who long ago were turned to dust.

The autumn leaves fall silently as tear filled eyes close tight,

We will not learn from war.

We will not learn what's right.

So cry, and speak his name so he will be remembered.

His bones now turned to dust, lie deep within the soil,

But up his spirit rose and now he flies,

Feel him in the wind as he caresses a cheek

And smile,

Yes, smile for the boy before the war

Who lived, and laughed and ran and played,

With brothers and sisters and friends and school,

With hope in his heart and girls in his mind,

And speak his name so he will be remembered.

The soft petals of the poppy that scatter in the breeze

Carry his dreams as he sleeps,

Shed tears for the man but smile for the boy

Who was happy.

Hear too his laughter in the wind as it dances in your ears and tickles,

Look for him in a song or as the sun rises up
And bathes the hills in its light,
And speak his name so he will be remembered.

# Mither tongue

A puckle o' Scots words mak nae sense ava,
Like rickmatick for affair or midder for yer ma,
Yer leg is yer shank and yer ear is yer lug,
Ye yowff doon yer tea and yer phizog's yer mug,
But dinna forhooie yer mither tongue,
It bides in yer hairt and there it has clung,
So hud on tae it ticht and spik yer leid,
Pass it on ta eyer bairnies, it's a' they need.

# To…

To sit in a chair, to listen to music,

To allow the mind to rest, to have the music flow over you,

To feel your emotions that lie deep within,

To recognise what those emotions are,

To hear an inner voice, to acknowledge it,

To decide to follow it, to take a chance,

To see where it takes you, to drink in change,

To observe a new way of being,

To be aware, to know another way,

To sing a new song, to dance another dance,

To feel deeply,

To smile.

# The storm

Sometimes it's hard to see, the positive side of things,

When stress, worry and problems, are what life casually brings,

It is easy to get bogged down, and to feel that you're alone,

As if all ideas of happiness, have just got up and flown.

But if we ride the storm, eventually it will pass,

Nothing lasts forever, and soon good things will amass,

So hold on in there you're not alone, others feel the same,

The sun will shine, but until then, learn to dance in the rain.

# The power of words

Words enable us to hurt and to soothe,

To explain and confuse,

To tell a story that evokes emotion from love, compassion and hope,

To fear, hatred and revulsion.

Every word pricking the imagination,

Allowing the reader or listener to see another world or a moment in time.

Vivid descriptions enabling the mind to see scenes of beauty or horror,

Words are an outlet: an outpouring of emotion.

A way of healing, a way to express an idea,

A sign that commands, a recipe that instructs,

A card that sends a message, a book that tells a story,

A note that asks a question, a sentence that changes lives,

A phrase that evokes a memory.

The power to heal and to harm,

To lose yourself in a book or a poem or a song.

Words, and the effect of those words, can live forever.

Words are treasured and wasted, held dear or spurned,

Words are withheld, opportunities missed, regrets made,

Words are used as weapons to hurt, to revenge, to kill feelings.

An hello that starts a relationship,

A goodbye that ends one,

Words that make us laugh

And words that make us cry.

Use words wisely.

To tell a truth, to tell a lie,

To judge, to preach,

To comfort, to console,

To ridicule, to humiliate,

To encourage, to praise,

To shout, to whisper,

To accuse, to blame

To forgive, to nurture,

To give hope and to love.

And when the tongue cannot speak,

A look can say a thousand words.

# To you

I wish I had a crystal ball to show you what lies ahead,

There you lie curled up in a ball, cocooned in the covers of your bed,

Where hope seems to have abandoned you and the darkness is closing in,

When saying hello takes so much effort and the tiredness is in your bones.

No longer believing that things can change or that anyone understands,

Where life is all consuming and just breathing is so damn hard,

When all you want is calmness and peace,

And for everything just to stop,

To be released from this living Hell: to live and not just exist.

To wonder what it would be like to live as others do,

Whose lives seem so much easier and don't walk like they're pushing through glue.

May I walk alongside you? Just you and I today,

Let us imagine just for a moment, that there's a future worth seeing, waiting for us just ahead.

I wonder what sights will behold us, what sensations we will feel,

Curiosity carrying us forward as a tiny bubble of something stirs deep inside,

An old forgotten sensation re awakening and coming alive.

Getting a sense of the ground beneath, be it grass or sand or soil,

Feeling the sun or wind upon your face, the tingling on your skin.

Allowing your mind, for a moment, to glimpse the path ahead,

Perhaps a sense of intrigue as to what lies around the bend.

The colours and light shift and change with each brave new step,

Slowly those hesitant, faltering steps begin to move away from now.

Now look, just ahead there, a tiny spark of light,

Can you feel its magnet, pulling tiny bubbles of life to the surface?

I wonder what it would feel like to touch a new beginning,

Imagine if you could hold it in your hands, protect and nurture it,

That future held in a safe embrace.

It's something uniquely precious that it only belongs to you,

Your mind remembers what it's like to be calm,

And you can bathe in that memory for a while,

Swim around in the pool of calmness, soaking in the sense of freedom.

As we walk together the world begins to open,

New sights and sounds and scents,

And so along the passage of time where today is a long time ago,

Who else has joined us now?

A partner, children, a depth of love unimagined before,

A loving home, a career you have carved,

A lifetime of experiences to be shared and passed on,

Memories made and cherished on this journey known as life.

And all because you chose to let me walk with you, to show you there's another way to navigate through life.

I'll always choose to walk with you, my name is Hope, I should have said.

I wish I had a crystal ball to show you what lies ahead.

# September

An Indian summer has walked through the door,
See how she sparkles and shimmers,
As her light reflects off the lochs and seas
And her heat kindles a mirage over the water.

Her colours are vibrant and the flowers smile,
As the bees continue their work,
The air is charged as lightning strikes
And autumn is forced to lurk.

She won't be here long and soon will leave,
So we must allow nature to continue,
As her skirts swish when she walks out the door,
Wave farewell as she bows and leaves with a
smile.

# Hello little bee

Hello little bee, do you know how important you are?

You buzz around the flowers, roaming near and far,

Collecting all the nectar, and dispersing all the pollen,

Pollinating all the crops, for us, the neglectful fallen.

Pesticides and drought, pollution and global warming,

Have decreased your numbers, and given us a warning,

You control the growth, and quality of vegetation,

Without your services, there will be devastation.

The availability and diversity, of fresh produce would decline,

And human nutrition, would greatly suffer over time,

We would lose the plants you pollinate, and the animals that eat them,

This would continue along the food chain, therefore the future would be grim.

Every living thing, would be affected by your loss,

The death of plants, animals and humans, would be the ultimate cost,

We need to stop and listen, to what the scientists say,

Otherwise our world is lost, that's the price we'll pay.

# Hello little fish

Hello little fish swimming in the sea,

Do you understand why our world is changing?

As you trudge through waste and plastics

And how their presence is so wide ranging.

When you ingest toxic substances that cause damage to your gills,

Causing you to haemorrhage over time,

Are you aware that the pollutants in your sea

Travel to your world from mine?

You see, us humans allow your world to become polluted by ours,

Chemicals, litter and waste pour into the sea and your environment sours,

The pollution changes the physical, chemical and biological state of your sea,

Threatening the ecosystems and humans ignore your plea.

You become entangled in bags and nets and eat plastic thinking it's prey,

You swim through human waste and toxins poison you every day.

But it goes full circle, you may be glad to hear,

Because when we eat you, we too ingest pollutants

That fact results in fear,

Fear of falling ill, contracting cancers or other health conditions,

We contaminate ourselves and have to live with our contrition.

# If dogs could speak

A litter of pups suckle their mother and you think how cute they are,

And the owner asks which one you would like to buy,

The law says you can take your chosen puppy from its mother in eight weeks,

To live in a house with humans, no pack with which to lie.

If dogs could speak what would they say and would you listen anyway?

One by one the pups are taken, sold into human hands,

To be kept as pets or for your company,

I wonder how that mother feels as she watches them being taken,

She has fed and groomed and played with them, loved them unconditionally.

If dogs could speak what would they say and would you listen anyway?

You put a collar round her neck, this tiny pup that now belongs to you,

And soon she learns the human rules in which there is no choice,

No choice of learning to hunt for food,

No choice to roam in hills and woods and find a mate with which to breed,

No choice to sleep where she feels safe or to bark as nature intended.

If dogs could speak what would they say and would you listen anyway?

I can hear the uproar as you shout – 'But she is loved!

I love that pet with all my heart and, Look! She is happy,

She greets me and gets excited when I walk in through the door.'

But you are forgetting – she knows no other life,

Had no choice in her captivity.

Had no choice to live as humans do.

If she could speak, what would she say, and would you listen anyway?

Would she say, I want to live with humans and not with a pack of dogs

Be fed dry food, walked on a lead and be forbidden from breeding,

And when I am allowed to breed it's with no partner of my choosing,

I am happy for my pups to be taken from me and sold,

I am glad you bought me and have me living in your home?

If she could speak, what would she say, and would you listen anyway?

Or would she say, Let me be free, free to roam and hunt as animals are meant to do,

To make my own choices and to bark without being shouted at,

Free from humans using me for their own selfish needs,

And free to teach my pups what they need to learn,

Freedom from captivity. Free to be a dog?

If she could speak, what would she say and would you listen anyway?

Would she say, Hear me! Find other ways to comfort yourselves.

Find other ways to do that job. Find other ways to be entertained,

Find other ways to master others,

I do not want to eat dry biscuits or wear coats as humans do,

Do not humiliate me with your 'cute' clothing,

Do not make me beg for food – to stand on my hind legs,

Do not have me dance or jump through hoops for you,

Do not use me to stave your loneliness?

If I could speak, what would I say and would you listen anyway?

# Do you ever wonder?

Do you ever wonder, as you look upon a cloud,

That if it could speak what it would say, to the land that it shrouds?

Would it call upon the trees, with their roots deep within the soil,

To plead to them to clean the air, in which they're forced to toil?

Would it ask the flowers if there's anything they can do,

To help the cloud breathe easier, as it looks upon the view?

Pushed and buffeted by the wind, is it friend or foe?

Could it take the cloud to better climes, than what it fears below?

Perhaps it will consult the animals, that roam far down below,

In the hope that they can explain, pollution in the air flow,

That rises up into the cloud, causing it to suffer,

Making it all the harder, for the cloud to be a buffer.

But of course it cannot speak, that cloud high in the air,

Protecting us and cooling us, from the strong sun's glare,

Each cloud lives but minutes, so there is no time,

To ask us humans, why we've crossed a line.

# Time

I had this thought that languished, in the recess of my mind,

That I would like to write a book, I had no idea what kind,

I would think of plots and stories, but little did I know,

That from the life of my great granny, a story would grow.

A story that encompassed, ghosts and fairies both,

I weaved a tale of Jane, to whom I pledged an oath,

I felt her hand rest over mine, she pulled the pen along,

Her words, they danced across the page, her presence ever strong.

I laughed at every funny part, and cried when it was sad,

It stirred my soul and filled my heart, and when it finished I was glad,

Glad that I now knew her, she nestled in my tale,

Jane had reached across the ages and pulled back the ancestor's veil.

For time has no real meaning, it's something we travel through,

And some have the ability to have another view,

To look into the future or see into the past,

The wonders of a world that we know nothing of, are vast.

That moment between wake and sleep, a shifting in the air,

That is where these wonders lie, look for them, they are there,

Those long now dead or not yet born, there is nothing to entail,

Embrace what's all around you.

Time is but a veil.

Printed in Great Britain
by Amazon

45522090R00047